OLD TESTAMENT

GEN Z

BIBLE STORIES

Jace Hunter

Copyright © by Jace Hunter 2024. All rights reserved.

Before this document is duplicated or reproduced in any manner, the publisher's consent must be gained. Therefore, the contents within can neither be stored electronically, transferred, nor kept in a database. Neither in Part nor full can the document be copied, scanned, faxed, or retained without approval from the publisher or creator.

Contents

IN THE BEGINNING

ADAM & EVE SPILL THE TEA IN EDEN

CAIN'S MAJOR SHADE THE FIRST GHOSTING

NOAH'S ARK

THE ULTIMATE RESCUE SQUAD

BABEL'S TOWER

ABRAHAM STANS GOD

ISAAC'S ALMOST OoF

JACOB'S GLOW-UP

JOSEPH'S TECHNICOLOR FLEX AND EPIC CLAPBACK

MOSES

THE RED SEA SPLIT

TEN COMMANDMENTS

JOSHUA & JERICHO WALLS

GIDEON'S GANG

SAMSON'S LOCKS

SAMUEL HEARS THE WHISPER CHALLENGE

DAVID VS. GOLIATH

KING SOLOMON WISDOM

ELIJAH'S FIRE

JONAH'S BIG FISH ENERGY

DANIEL'S LION'S DEN

ESTHER'S TEA

#NEHEMIAH'S BUILD BACK BETTER

TL; DR (TOO LONG; DIDN'T READ)

GLOSSARY

IN THE BEGINNING

Genesis chapter 1

Yo, peeps, let's spill the celestial tea. In the very first drop of time, the universe was like, totally ghosting—no snaps, no stories, nada. But then, the Big G (you know, God) decided it was time to glow up the cosmos.

First thing's first, the Almighty hit up the void with a "Let there be light," and bam! It was like the ultimate room makeover. And God wasn't about that mix-up life; He split the light from the dark—called it day and night. That's a 24-hour cycle, peeps, the original round-the-clock vibe.

Next up, God's like, "Let's make a sky," 'cause earth needed that top-tier ceiling. He straight-up yeeted a dome between the waters, calling it sky. Talk about raising the roof, am I right?

Day three, God's scrolling through the barren land and hits it with the ultimate green thumb action. Land, seas, plants, and trees started popping up like nature's first influencers. Earth's feed was getting all the aesthetic goals.

Cue day four, and God's planning the 'gram for the sky. He launches the sun for those daytime feels and the moon for the after-hours mood. Stars got added to the mix 'cause the night sky's gotta flex that bling.

Big G wasn't done. Day five was for the water and sky glow-up. He filled the sea with fish that could've won any fin-fluencer award and the sky with birds to start the original Twitter.

On the sixth day, God rolled out the land squad. Animals of all types started trending, from #CuteCuddly to #FierceAF. But the Creator wasn't about to ghost just yet. He crafted humans, the real VIPs. He's like, "Go forth, be lit, and keep it 100."
After all that crafting, even the Almighty needed a self-care day. So, on day seven, God hit pause, blessed the day, and made it the OG day of rest. All about that balance, you know?

And that's how the universe got its clout. From the OG light drop to the debut of humans, it was the most epic start-up ever. So when you're out here, living your best life, remember the Big G's six-day glow-up that gave us this YOLO existence. Stay woke to the wonders, fam.

ADAM & EVE SPILL THE TEA IN EDEN

Genesis chapter 2

Yo fam, let's dive into how the first humans, Adam and Eve, totally spilled the celestial tea in the Garden of Eden, which was basically the OG luxury resort crafted by the Big Boss Himself.

So, God had just finished decking out the Earth with all the fixings: trees that were both snackable and Snapchat-worthy, rivers flowing with that clear, blue #NoFilter look, and animals vibing in peace. Adam was living his best life, naming animals like it was NBD, but God peeped that Adam was rolling solo and was like, "Nah, fam, let's get you a partner."

God then hit Adam with the deepest nap ever, snagged a rib, and—boom!—Eve entered the chat, the first-ever glow-up from a rib. And Adam? He was totally shook, like "Bone of my bones, flesh of my flesh," calling her 'woman' because she was the remix of 'man.'

Now, Eden had this one tree, right? The tree of the knowledge of good and evil. And God was super clear: "Everything in this garden is fair game, but that tree? That's the unsubscribe button from this paradise life." But then, this crafty serpent slid into Eve's DMs and was like, "You won't actually take the L if you eat from that tree. You'll just be woke, like God, knowing all the tea."

Eve peeped the fruit, and it looked like a straight-up snack. She thought, "Bet, let's get that knowledge."

She took a bite and passed it to Adam, who didn't even hesitate. The second they ate it, their eyes popped open, and they realized they were in their birthday suits. Major oof!

They tried to DIY some fig leaf fits and played hide-and-seek with God. But you can't ghost the Creator, right? When God rolled up, He was like, "What's this mess?" Adam and Eve spilled the whole tea, blaming each other and the serpent. Classic blame game.

Because they went against the one rule, God had to hit them with the hard logout from Eden. Pain, work, and struggle became the new grind, and cherubim with a flaming sword got the gig to keep them from the tree of life.

So that's the real tea on Adam and Eve. They had one job, but got tempted to hit up the forbidden, and ended up with the first major plot twist in human history. It was all about choices, consequences, and knowing that some tea... might just be too hot to handle.

CAIN'S MAJOR SHADE THE FIRST GHOSTING

Genesis chapter 4

Alright squad, buckle up for the OG sibling rivalry that turned into the first ghosting incident in human history. We're talking about Cain and Abel, the first bros to ever walk the earth.

Cain was all about that farm life, growing veggies and whatnot, while Abel was the shepherd, flexing with the fluffiest sheep on the 'gram. When it was time to drop likes for the Big G, they both brought their A-game.

Abel brought the firstborn of his flock, the real VIP sheep. Cain, though, he just grabbed some random fruits of his labor. No cap, God was vibing with Abel's offering more, and Cain? He was salty AF.

God hit up Cain like, "Bro, why the long face? Do well, and you'll be chillin'. But if you're sleeping on doing right, sin's at your door, and it's got your number." Cain was supposed to catch the hint and level up his game, but he was low-key plotting.

Cain was all, "Yo Abel, let's bounce to the fields." Abel, thinking it's just bro time, went along. But when they were out of God's Wi-Fi range, Cain went full dark mode and yeeted Abel from the earth. Major betrayal alert.

God came through and was like, "Where's your brother at, Cain?" Cain tried to play it cool with, "Am I my brother's keeper?" But God's got all the receipts. He knew what's up and called Cain out on the carpet for spilling Abel's tea all over the ground. Because Cain decided to throw the ultimate shade, God was like, "You're canceled from the ground, bro." Cain got the boot, becoming a restless wanderer—a ghost of his former self.

And that's the story of how Cain threw major shade and ghosted his own brother. Abel's out, Cain's wandering, and the world's got its first lesson in why ghosting is, like, seriously not cool. Keep it 100, don't let the jealousy bug bite, and remember, fam, your actions always leave a text history.

NOAH'S ARK

THE ULTIMATE RESCUE SQUAD

Genesis chapter 7

Alright, fam, let's spill the tea on the most epic save-the-animals challenge ever to hit planet Earth. We're talking about Noah, his fam, and a whole lot of furry + feathery + whatever-y friends.

So here's the sitch: Humanity was acting all kinds of sus, and the Earth was straight-up not having a good time. The vibes were terrible, 0/10 would not recommend. God peeped this hot mess and was like, "Reset button, where you at?"

Enter Noah, this righteous dude who was basically Earth's last hope. God gave him the pro gamer move: "Build an ark, fam, 'cause we're about to cleanse the cache with a flood that's got more coverage than your fave influencer."

Noah got to work, stacking wood planks like he was playing the most intense game of Minecraft IRL. This ark was yuge—think Titanic but with less romance and more livestock.

Once the ark was 100, God was like, "Noah, it's go time." Noah got his fam and animals on board, two by two. It was like the world's first BOGO deal, but for survival. And these animals weren't just from the local petting zoo. We're talking lions, tigers, bears—oh my!

The skies opened up like someone smashed the 'pour' button on the world's biggest Super Soaker. It rained for a hot minute—or, well, 40 days and 40 nights, which is a lot of minutes. The whole Earth was swimming, except for Noah and his floating zoo. They floated on that ark for what felt like forever, probably binge-watching the waves and getting to know every animal's life story. Noah sent out a raven and then a dove to scope if it was time to drop anchor. The dove brought back an olive branch, which was basically the ancient version of a green light.

When the waters finally chilled, the ark squad said, "Thank you, next" to the boat life. They stepped out onto dry land, and it was like the biggest group stretch after the longest Netflix marathon ever.

God was all about that promise life, so He threw a rainbow in the sky as the OG peace sign—a reminder that He wouldn't flood the Earth like that again.

And that's the deets on Noah's Ark, the ultimate rescue squad. Noah kept it 100 with the faithfulness, the animals were saved, and humanity got a reboot. Remember, when life's flooding you with drama, sometimes you gotta build your own ark and ride it out. Keep your squad close and look out for those rainbows.

BABEL'S TOWER

WHEN FLEXING GOES WRONG

Genesis chapter 11

Alright, time to spill the real tea about when humanity decided to flex too hard and ended up with the ultimate connection error—talking about the Tower of Babel, folks.

So peeps were feeling themselves, speaking the same language, and they hit up the plains of Shinar. They were like, "Let's do the most and build a city with a tower that's straight fire, touching the sky, 'cause we're that good." It was all about that clout life, chasing fame like it was a drop from their fave brand.

These early influencers didn't just want any old tower; they wanted the deluxe edition. They swapped out stones for bricks—total glow-up material—and used tar for mortar. 'Cause who needs nature when you've got the tech to make things extra AF?

But upstairs, God clocked their little DIY project and wasn't about to let them turn Earth into a game of who's got the biggest ego. So, He came down for a divine reality check.

God saw their tower, and He knew this was just the start. With everyone on the same wavelength, the flex could only get more extra. So, He hit them with the biggest plot twist: scrambling their comms. Suddenly, everyone's talking in TikTok captions, and no one's understanding the vibe check.

It was pure chaos. Imagine trying to collab on a project when one's speaking in memes, another's all about that hashtag life, and someone else is stuck on Vine references. Yeah, it was a mess. The tower project got ghosted, and everyone scattered across the globe, forming their own cliques with peeps who could understand their new slang.

The city got dubbed "Babel" because that's where God mixed up the squad's chat. It was the day humanity learned that sometimes trying to slide into the DMs of the heavens just gets you left on read.

And that's the lowdown on Babel's Tower, where the world's biggest flex turned into a crash course in diversity. It's like God was saying, "Stay humble, don't clout-chase, and remember: the best connections are about understanding, not just being the loudest in the room."

ABRAHAM STANS GOD

THE OG PROMISE

Genesis chapter 12

Okay, fam, let's throw it back to the days of dusty sandals and epic faith. We're talking about Abraham, the dude who stanned God so hard, he became the blueprint for loyalty programs.

First up, God slid into Abram's life (yeah, he was Abram before the rebrand) and was like, "Leave your zip code, your fam's house, and your father's Netflix account. I'm about to take you to a place that slaps harder than any influencer's vacay spot."

God promised Abram the ultimate follower count: "I'll make you the father of a whole nation, like if your descendants were stars, you wouldn't be able to keep track—no cap." And Abram, who hadn't even hit the big 1-0-0 in age, was down. He didn't even ask for a blue check beside his name.

Abram and his crew packed up their camels and yeeted out of Haran, cruising over to Canaan. Even when the GPS was sketchy, and the food pics were just basic unleavened bread, Abram trusted God's plan. No FOMO, just faith.

Years later, God's like, "I haven't forgotten you, fam. You're gonna have so many kids, they'll be like the OG viral content." God went all in, changing Abram's handle to Abraham, which basically means "Big Poppa of Many." And Sarai? She leveled up to Sarah, 'cause she was about to be the mother of nations.

There was no pinky promise here. God was all about that covenant life. He asked Abraham to flex the faith by marking it on the fam—a little snip-snip action that would set them apart as the chosen squad.

Later, when Abraham was big chillin' at 99, God dropped the news: "You and Sarah are about to have a baby." And Abraham LOL'd, 'cause, like, they were practically ancient. But when Isaac hit the scene, it was clear—God keeps it 100.

And that's the story of how Abraham stanned God before it was even a thing. Dude was the original hype man for the man upstairs, showing us that sometimes you gotta step out and vibe with the divine to hit that promised legacy. Keep your squad tight, your promises tighter, and your faith the tightest.

ISAAC'S ALMOST OoF

TRUST AT 100

Genesis chapter 22

Yo, let's unpack the saga of Isaac, whose life got more intense than a season finale cliffhanger. This is the tale of mad trust and an almost oof that had everyone on edge.

So Abraham, the OG dad of faith, gets the ultimate DM from God: "Take your son, your only son whom you vibe with, Isaac, and yeet up to Moriah. Imma show you the spot to offer him up." Talk about a test that's more hardcore than any TikTok challenge.

Abraham's like, "Bet," but internally, he's gotta be sweating 'cause this ask is next level. He and Isaac load up the wood, fire up the Yeezys (or, you know, whatever the ancient kicks were), and start the most sus hike ever.

Isaac's carrying the wood like a champ, but then he clocks the no-sheep situation. "Yo, Pops, we got the fire and wood, but where's the lamb for the burn?" And Abraham, with trust so high it's in another stratosphere, hits back, "God will provide the sheep for the burn, my guy."

They get to the spot, and Abraham builds an altar. Isaac's still thinking a sheep's about to pop out like some divine surprise party, but then he's the one getting laid on the altar. It's all getting a bit too real.

Just as Abraham's about to go through with it, an angel yeets into the scene, yelling, "Hold up, Abraham! You've proved your loyalty is legit." And there, in the bushes, a ram is just chilling, ready to take Isaac's place. Major relief—like finding out your fave show got renewed.

This whole wild ride was a trust fall exercise, and Abraham and Isaac passed with flying colors. They named the place "The Lord Will Provide," 'cause when you're at the end of your rope, that's when the plot twists.

And so, Isaac's almost oof became the ultimate trust flex. The fam walked away from that mountain with a story wilder than any viral vid. It's all about that faith, fam—keeping it 100, even when you're staring at the impossible. Trust level: biblical.

JACOB'S GLOW-UP

DREAMING BIG AND SCHEMING BIGGER

Genesis chapter 27

Grab your tea, fam, 'cause we're about to spill on Jacob, the ultimate dreamer and schemer whose life was more rollercoaster than your last relationship status.

So Jacob was born clutching his twin bro Esau's heel, basically saying "Catch me if you can" from the womb. Esau was all about that outdoorsy life, while Jacob was the quiet type, probs would've been a TikTok e-boy if he could.

One day, Esau came back from the wild, hangry like you wouldn't believe, and Jacob was chef'ing up some top-tier stew. Esau was like, "Bruh, let me smash that stew." Jacob, seeing the ultimate leverage moment, was like, "Trade you your birthright for this bowl?" And Esau, not thinking straight, was like "Yeet, it's yours," for a bowl of the good stuff. Major oops.

Fast forward, and their dad Isaac's eyes were like, "I can't even," almost blind. He told Esau to whip up some delish game meat, planning to drop a blessing on him. But their mom, Rebekah, overheard and plotted with Jacob to snag that blessing.

Jacob went full cosplay, dressing up in Esau's clothes and putting on goat-skin gloves (for that authentic hairy vibe), and brought Isaac the food. Isaac, none the wiser, spilled a primo blessing on Jacob, thinking he was Esau. When Esau found out, the drama hit the fan, and Jacob had to dip out faster than a cancelled YouTuber.

While on the run, Jacob crashed in a random spot and had a dream where a ladder connected Earth to Heaven, with angels doing the up-and-down routine. God stood there and hit Jacob with promises of land and blessings, making his lineage more spread out than WiFi signals.

Jacob woke up all hype, saying, "Surely the Lord is in this place, and I was sleeping on it!" He turned his stone pillow into a memorial pillar and named the place Bethel, or "House of God." He vowed that if God stuck with him, he'd stan God forever and give back a solid tenth of everything.

And that's how Jacob went from homebody to heavenly-connected big shot. His glow-up was messy, filled with dreams and drama, but it started him on a path to becoming Israel, a name that slaps harder than any influencer's rebrand. So keep your eyes on the stars and your schemes on the DL, 'cause you never know when a glow-up might be just a dream away.

JOSEPH'S TECHNICOLOR FLEX AND EPIC CLAPBACK

Genesis chapter 37

Strap in, fam, 'cause we're about to dive into the saga of Joseph, the dreamboat turned CEO, who had more drip than a viral ice bucket challenge.

Joseph was his pops Jacob's fave, no cap. He got gifted this wild, colorful flex coat that made his bros salty 'cause it screamed "Dad's fave." Joseph also had these wild dreams of being the top dog, and he didn't hit mute when telling his bros. Not the smoothest move.

His bros were so heated, they plotted the ultimate cancel move. They threw Joseph into a pit and were gonna leave him on read, forever. But then they thought, "Why not secure the bag?" So they sold him to some Ishmaelite influencers passing through.

Joseph got taken to Egypt and ended up as Potiphar's right-hand man. Dude was blessed with the Midas touch, until Potiphar's wife tried to slide into his DMs. When he left her on read, she framed him with the ultimate screenshot, and Joseph got sent to the king's private server (aka prison).

Even in the clink, Joseph's dream skills were legit. He decoded dreams for some of Pharaoh's former crew, and word got out. When Pharaoh had some mind-bending dreams, Joseph got summoned for the ultimate collab.

Joseph spilled the tea on Pharaoh's dreams—seven years of #Blessed harvests followed by seven years of #Cursed famine. Pharaoh was shook and made

Joseph his main man, the prime minister of grain and game. Talk about a promotion.

Fast forward, and the famine hit hard. Joseph's bros showed up in Egypt looking for a grocery drop. They didn't recognize Joseph, who was now rocking the Egyptian influencer aesthetic. After some cat-and-mouse games and a full-on emotional reveal, the fam had the ultimate reunion.

Joseph hit them with the "you meant evil, but God meant it for good" line. For real, he saved the day, securing bags of grain for the region and his fam. The bro who once flexed too hard with a coat was now flexing wisdom and forgiveness.

And there you have it, the story of Joseph's high-key

flex and low-key clapback, serving lessons in drip and

dreams. He went from the bros' least fave TikTok to Egypt's verified account. So remember, when the haters try to cancel you, just keep your head up and your coat colorful. You might just end up running the show.

MOSES

PHAROAH'S CANCELED, LET MY PEOPLE GO

Exodus chapter 2

Gear up, 'cause it's storytime about Moses, the ultimate influencer who used his platform to throw the biggest "bye, Felicia" to tyranny.

It all started when Pharaoh was being extra, issuing the ultimate toxic command to yeet Hebrew baby boys. Moses' mom wasn't about that life, so she crafted a DIY baby yacht and sent Moses down the Nile, like a VIP in a floating crib.

Baby Moses got scooped up by Pharaoh's daughter, who was on her daily self-care river stroll. She was like, "Imma keep him," and Moses got that palace glow-up. Talk about a rags-to-riches Snap story.

Fast forward, and Moses dipped from Egypt after things got heated. He was living that shepherd life when the Big G slid into his DMs via a burning bush that was all flame, no char. God was like, "Moses, you're the chosen one to slide into Egypt and tell Pharaoh 'hashtag let my people go.'"

Pharaoh was on that stubborn vibe, so God started dropping plagues like they were diss tracks. We're talking rivers turning to Yeezy red, flexing frogs, swarms of bugs with more buzz than a viral tweet, and a whole lineup of other not-so-pleasant releases.

Even after all that, Pharaoh was still sleeping on Moses' requests. So God rolled out the final play: the Passover. Hebrew fams threw lamb's blood on the doorframe, which was the ancient version of "Do Not Disturb." The angel of death passed over these cribs, but Egypt got hit with the ultimate sorrow.

Pharaoh finally hit "unsubscribe" and let the Hebrews bounce. But plot twist: he rage-quit and chased after them. Moses, with that staff clout, parted the Red Sea like it was the crowd at a Kanye concert. Hebrews walked through on dry land, and when Pharaoh's squad tried it, they got the full wash cycle.

After the sea closed up like a deleted tweet, Moses and the freed squad spent 40 years wandering the desert—a journey longer than any Snapchat streak. But they eventually got to flex in the Promised Land, which was the ultimate group chat destination.

So that's the tea on Moses, the original freedom fighter, and social justice warrior. He had the faith to see "Read" receipts from God and the boldness to tell a tyrant, "You're cancelled. Let my people go." Stay woke, fam, and never be afraid to stand up to the pharaohs in your life.

THE RED SEA SPLIT

ISRALITES DIPPED OUT

Exodus chapter 15

Yo, let's rewind and hit the play button on one of the most epic mic-drops in history. We're talking Moses, the Israelites, and a sea that decided to split like it was dodging paparazzi.

So the Israelites were fresh outta Egypt, thinking they're about to start that free life, but Pharaoh was trippin' and sent the chariots to hunt 'em down. The crew was shook, caught between a rock, a hard place, and a whole lot of water.

Moses was standing there with the sea in front, haters behind, and God's promise in his DMs. The people were freaking out, but Moses was like, "Stay chill, fam. Watch God do His thing."

Then Moses stretched out his staff, and God hit the Red Sea with the ultimate flex. That water split like the crowd at a concert when the headliner walks through. Walls of water on the left, walls of water on the right, and dry land down the middle. Mind. Blown.

The Israelites didn't need to be told twice. They dipped out across the seabed, probably filming the first-ever "Walking on Dry Land Challenge" in history.

Pharaoh's squad saw the open lane and thought, "Bet, let's chase 'em." But just as Israel hit the other side and Moses copped the staff, the sea came crashing down like the world's worst belly flop.

Pharaoh's army got swallowed up like a deleted scene, and the Israelites knew God wasn't playing games.

On the far shore, the Israelites were living for their newfound freedom. They threw down the biggest thanksgiving TikTok ever, with Miriam leading the dance challenge, tambourines and all.

And that's the deets on the Red Sea's epic split where the Israelites dipped out in style. It was the day when a whole nation learned that when God says He's got you, He's got you. So when you're up against it, remember the Red Sea remix – sometimes, the only way out is through, and it might just be on dry land.

TEN COMMANDMENTS

GOD'S ULTIMATE DMs

Exodus chapter 34

Slide into the scene where the Israelites are camping out at Mount Sinai, post-epic sea split, and God's about to slide into Moses' DMs with the ultimate listicle.

God called Moses up Mount Sinai for a one-on-one, leaving the Israelites to chill at base camp. Up there, Moses got the lowdown, and it wasn't just 280 characters—this was stone tablet territory.

God dropped the Ten Commandments, the rules to keep the Israelites' feed clean and their community game strong:

1. No Copy-Paste Gods - "I'm your number one, no screenshotting other gods. Keep it original."

2. No Faking the Funk - "Don't craft idols. I'm beyond that 3D printer life. Worship the Creator, not the created."

3. Handle the Name with Care - "My name's not for your bloopers reel. Use it with respect."

4. The Rest Flex- "Sundays are for self-care, fam. Work hard for six days, then hit pause."

5. Fam First - "Honor the parentals. They're your OG support squad."

6. Life is Precious - "Don't end the life game. All lives are premium content."

7. Stay Loyal - "Relationship status should be 'committed,' not 'it's complicated.'"

8. Hands Off - "If it's not in your inventory, don't pocket it. Stealing's a bad look."

9. Keep It 100 - "Don't spill fake tea. Stay truthful, no catfishing."

10. Don't Crave the Rave - "Keep your eyes on your own paper. Wanting what others have is a no-go."

Moses came down from the mountain with the tablets, the OG Terms of Service for a blessed life. The Israelites had to agree to the terms to keep the connection with God strong and unbuffered.

And there you have it, the Ten Commandments, aka

God's Ultimate DMs, carved in stone so the message

wouldn't get lost in translation. It's the blueprint for keeping your soul's profile on point and your community thriving. So when you're scrolling through life, remember the OG status updates from the mountaintop—they're timeless.

JOSHUA & JERICHO WALLS

THAT SOUND THO

Joshua chapter 6

Time to hit play on the ultimate surround-sound story that had walls dropping faster than a viral dance challenge. We're talking Joshua, a city called Jericho, and a playlist so powerful it made history.

Joshua, the new leader on the block after Moses dipped, sent a couple of spies to scope out Jericho. They were low-key about it, but they still got clocked. Rahab, the MVP innkeeper, hid them and helped them escape, securing her spot in the hall of fame.

God hit up Joshua with a strategy that was more out there than an abstract TikTok trend. "March around the city with all your soldiers, make no sound, do this for six days. On the seventh, it's gonna be lit."

So Joshua and his crew did just that. They went full silent mode around Jericho once a day, the priests carrying the Ark and blowing trumpets. Jericho peeps were probably watching from the walls like, "What's this new challenge?"

On the seventh day, the Israelites went full Coachella around Jericho—not once, but seven times. And at Joshua's cue, the priests dropped the sickest trumpet beat, and everyone shouted like they were at the final countdown on New Year's Eve.

And fam, you won't believe it unless you were there, but those walls just yeeted themselves out of existence. They crumbled like a bad cookie recipe, and the Israelites swarmed in like it was Black Friday.

Jericho was theirs, and they kept their word to Rahab. The city got the left swipe, completely destroyed—except for Rahab and her fam, who got the verified survival badge.

And that's the 411 on Joshua and the OG sound wave demolition. Jericho's walls didn't stand a chance against that divine bass drop. So when you're facing your own walls, just remember: sometimes the win comes from sticking to the plan and waiting for that sound tho.

GIDEON'S GANG

LOWKEY HEROES

Judges chapter 6

Lock in, 'cause we're about to unpack the tale of Gideon, the underdog who became leader of the most lowkey lit squad ever to take the battlefield.

Israel was playing hide-and-seek with the Midianites, who were majorly griefing their servers. Then, an angel pulled up to Gideon, who was lowkey threshing wheat and minding his own biz, and was like, "God's got you on His fantasy team, champ."

Gideon was all, "Imma need some proof," because he wasn't about to step up without a sign. So he put out a fleece, asking for some morning dew magic—wet fleece, dry ground, then vice versa. And what do you know? God came through. It was a real-life "expectation vs. reality" that actually matched up.

Gideon rallied his troops, but God was about to play the ultimate battle royale. He told Gideon, "Your squad's too thicc. Let's slim it down." After a couple of rounds of divine matchmaking, Gideon's army went from a whole festival crowd to an exclusive VIP party.

Armed with just torches, jars, and trumpets—like they were heading to the most intense candlelit vigil ever—Gideon's gang of 300 surrounded the Midianite camp at night. This was no ASMR session, though.

On Gideon's cue, the gang smashed their jars, flashed their torches, and blew on their trumpets like they were dropping the bass at a concert. They shouted, "For the Lord and for Gideon!" so loud, the

Midianites woke up shook, started wilding out, and turned on each other.

With the Midianites in self-destruct mode, Gideon's gang went in. The stragglers got chased down, and the leaders got served. Israel got the W without even swinging a sword.

And that's the story of Gideon's Gang, the lowkey heroes who played it cool and let the noise do the work. They went from zero to legends with just some jars, some horns, and a whole lot of faith. Remember, it ain't always about the size of the squad, but the size of the courage in the squad. Keep it stealthy, keep it faithful, and let the haters defeat themselves.

SAMSON'S LOCKS

STRENGTH GONE VIRAL

Judges chapter 14

Gather 'round for the deets on Samson, the original influencer with a power-up haircare routine that had everyone double-tapping.

Before Samson could even swipe right on life, an angel hit up his parents with some divine terms and conditions. He was to be a Nazirite from birth—no razor buzzcuts, just pure, uncut flow. His locks were the source of some serious gains, making him stronger than any gym beast.

One day, Samson was out and about when a lion tried to jump scare him. But Samson, armed with nothing but those holy follicles, tore it apart like it was a wet paper bag. It was so lowkey, he didn't even Snapchat it. Later, he turned the lion's carcass into a bee Airbnb, 'cause why not?

At his wedding feast, Samson dropped a riddle on the Philistines, betting them some sweet threads if they could solve it. But they were playing on easy mode 'cause they got his wife to spill the tea. Samson paid up in a rage-quit moment, delivering the clothes after a quick farm raid.

When his wife got nexted by his best man, Samson went full savage mode. He tied foxes two by two, set their tails on fire, and sent them through the Philistine fields like the world's worst gender reveal party.

Enter Delilah, the OG thirst trap, who got the Philistines to sponsor her for the deets on Samson's power source. After some failed attempts and a lot of nagging, Samson finally caved and let slip about his no-cut contract.

While Samson was catching Zs, Delilah went full barber, and the Philistines swooped in. Power level dropped to zero, and they captured our guy, putting him on blind mode and making him grind grain like a common noob.

But those holy locks started respawning. During a Philistine flex-fest with Samson as the main event, he prayed for that one last power-up. Leaning on the temple pillars, he brought the house down—literally—turning the party into a pancake stack.

And that's the saga of Samson's Locks, where strength went viral but ended with a major plot twist. His story's a cautionary tweet: your power ain't in the clout, it's in staying true to your roots—hair or otherwise. Keep your secrets locked down, and don't let anyone trim your potential.

RUTH LOYALTY

Ruth chapter 1

Let's get into the heartwarming saga of Ruth, the Moabite queen of loyalty, who showed us that sometimes, family isn't just the one you're born with—it's the one you choose.

So, Naomi and her fam left Bethlehem because the food sitch was looking sus and settled in Moab. Fast forward, and Naomi's husband and sons are logged out of life, leaving her with two daughters-in-law, Ruth and Orpah.

Naomi, feeling all the feels and FOMO about her hometown, decides to yeet back to Bethlehem. She's like, "Go back to your mom's house. Thank you, next." Orpah hits the tears and bounces, but Ruth? She's on that ride-or-die vibe.

Ruth claps back with the ancient world's most retweetable line: "Where you go, I go; where you stay, I stay; your people are my people, and your God, my God." That's the kind of loyalty that doesn't just pop up in your 'Best Friends' Stories.

They roll up in Bethlehem, and Ruth's hustle is fierce. She's out there gleaning in the fields, picking up leftover grain like it's Black Friday deals. And who owns the field? Boaz, the low-key bachelor and relative of Naomi's late hubby.

Boaz peeps Ruth working hard and hears about her loyalty. He's impressed—like, sharing-your-private-story impressed. He tells his workers to leave extra grain for her to pick up. That's ancient-world flirting, FYI.

Naomi, playing matchmaker, tells Ruth to freshen up and hit up Boaz on the threshing floor after he's had a bit to drink. Ruth does just that, uncovering his feet (code for, "Hey, I'm single and ready to mingle"). Boaz wakes up, sees Ruth, and it's a match made in heaven.

Boaz goes to town the next day to clear it with the closer relative, but the dude passes on Naomi's land. Boaz is like, "Bet, I'll redeem it," and marries Ruth. They have a son, Obed, who's the granddaddy of King David, making Ruth an OG in Jesus' family tree.

And that's Ruth's loyalty for you—ultimate squad goals. She stuck with Naomi through the worst, worked her fingers to the bone, and ended up in the lineage of royalty. So when you're thinking about your squad, remember: it's not about the followers; it's about the family you form along the way. Keep it 100, keep it loyal.

SAMUEL HEARS THE WHISPER CHALLENGE

1 Samuel 3

Alright, let's unbox the story of Samuel, the kiddo who had God sliding into his earbuds with a whisper challenge that was no game.

Samuel's living his best life at the temple with Eli, the high priest, because his mom, Hannah, was like, "God answered my DM, so I'll lend Samuel to Him." One night, Samuel's catching Zs when a voice hits him up, calling his name.

Thinking it's Eli on the night shift, Samuel yeets over to him like, "You rang?" But Eli's just as confused as someone getting a 'u up?' text from an unknown number. He sends Samuel back to bed, no read receipts.

This happens not once, not twice, but thrice. And each time, Samuel's sprinting to Eli, and Eli's like, "Bruh, wasn't me." But by the third time, Eli's got the notification. He realizes it's God trying to connect with Samuel.

Eli tells Samuel, "Next time, say 'Speak, for your servant is listening.'" So Samuel heads to bed, and sure enough, God hits him up again. Samuel drops the line, and God spills the celestial tea about what's gonna go down with Eli and his sons.

Come sunrise, Samuel's got that 'I know something you don't know' look. Eli, who's got a feeling he's about to be subtweeted by God, asks Samuel to spill. Samuel does, and it's a bitter brew: Eli's fam is about to be unfollowed by God because of some shady stuff they did.

Samuel grows up to be the legit voice of God, the prophet who's keeping it real in Israel. He's like God's verified account, no fake news, dropping truth bombs and anointing kings.

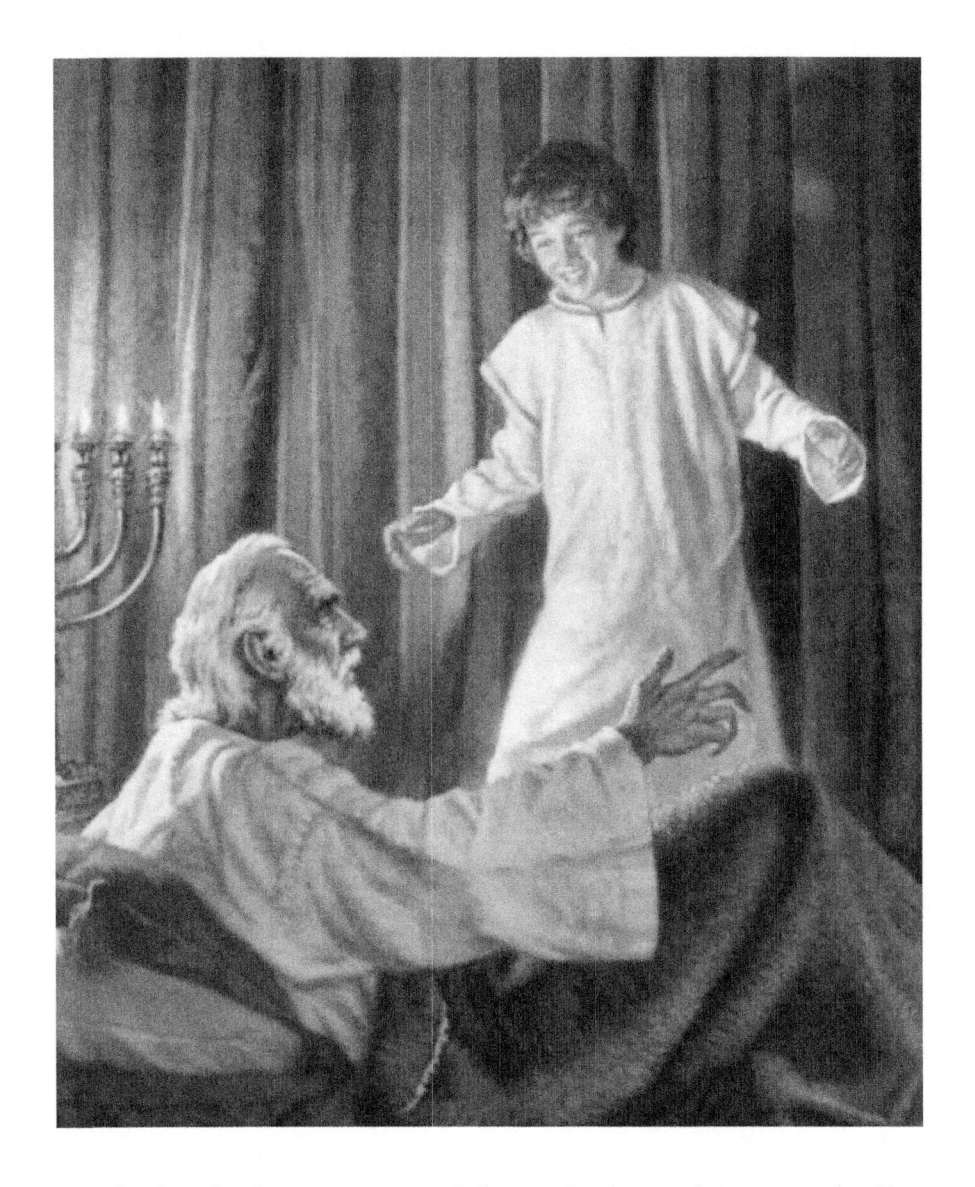

And that's how Samuel heard the whisper challenge and stepped up his game to prophet status. He showed us when God's calling, you don't leave Him on read. You listen up, 'cause that convo could be the one that changes your life's timeline. Keep your notifications on, fam.

DAVID VS. GOLIATH

THE ULTIMATE GLOW-UP

1 samuel 17

Peep this epic throwdown where young David went from shepherd to legend, snagging the victory royale against the OG troll, Goliath.

Goliath was this giant flexing on the Israelites daily, talking smack with a voice that could drop a beat. Dudes were shook, 'cause facing him was like going up against a final boss with no cheat codes.

Enter David, the freshest face on the scene, delivering DoorDash to his bros on the frontline. He peeps Goliath's trash talk and is all, "Who's this clown thinking he can ghost God's squad?"

King Saul hears David's got the guts and offers him the royal armor. But David's like, "Nah, fam, I can't even move in this." He knew his strength wasn't in the drip but in the divine.

David hits up a stream and scoops up five smooth stones—his version of a power-up. He's got his sling, his faith, and probably a fire playlist going as he steps up to the giant.

Goliath comes at David with the heavyweight trash talk, but David claps back with, "You come with swords, but I roll with God." Then he launches a rock from his sling with that aimbot precision, and it's a one-hit KO—Goliath's down for the count.

The Philistines see their hype man's been deleted, and they rage-quit the battlefield. Israelites go wild, 'cause their boy David just secured the dub without even drawing a sword.

David's glow-up was instant. From shepherd to soldier to social media sensation overnight. Saul's got him on speed dial, and it's only a matter of time before he's the one wearing the crown.

So that's the story of David vs. Goliath: The Ultimate Glow-Up. Little shepherd boy shows up and shuts down the giant with a pebble and some serious faith. It's the ultimate reminder to slide into your battles with confidence, 'cause with the right aim and a little help from above, you're undefeatable. Stay slinging, fam.

KING SOLOMON WISDOM

BRAINS OVER BRAWN

1 Kings 3

Time to get woke on King Solomon, the man who had more wisdom in his pinky than most had in their whole squad.

It all started with a dream where God was like, "Whatchu want?" Instead of asking for clout, long life, or the demise of his haters, Solomon went for the big brain play. He asked for wisdom to lead his people like a boss. God was so hyped at the request, He threw in riches and honor as bonus loot.

Solomon's wisdom got put to the test when two moms came through, beefing over a baby. Both claimed to be the legit mom, and things were getting more heated than a Twitter feud.

Solomon, in his big brain energy, was like, "Bet. Let's just split the baby in two and call it a day." The real mom showed her hand real quick, begging the king to give the other woman the baby instead of going through with the cut.

Solomon hit 'em with the plot twist, exposing the true mom and reuniting her with her kiddo. The kingdom was shook at the wisdom flex and knew this king was about to change the game.

Solomon's reign was like a golden age highlight reel. He built a temple that was #HouseGoals, penned some Proverbs that slapped, and even dropped some songs. Kings and queens from all over slid into Israel just to hear him spill facts.

And that's the story of King Solomon, the guy who chose wisdom and ended up with everything else. His brain was his brawn, and it scored him legendary status. So when life hits you with a choice, remember: flex the mind, and the gains will follow. Stay wise, peeps.

ELIJAH'S FIRE

PROPHETS THROWING SHADE

1 Kings 18

Get ready for the ultimate "my God is greater than yours" battle, where Elijah came through with the receipts and left everyone's jaw on the floor.

Elijah, tired of the Israelites' flip-flop fandom, threw down the gauntlet at Mount Carmel like, "Let's see whose follow count is real." He summoned the prophets of Baal for the ultimate showdown.

Elijah went before the people and said, "How long will you waver between two opinions? If the Lord is God, follow him; but if Baal is God, follow him." But the people said nothing.

The Baal squad was up first, setting up their altar and hollering for fire all day. They danced, they shouted, they even hit up the emo playlist, but nada. Elijah served up some premium shade, "Maybe shout louder? Perhaps he's deep in the group chat or just ghosting you."

At noon Elijah began to taunt them. "Shout louder!" he said. "Surely he is a god! Perhaps he is deep in thought, or busy, or traveling. Maybe he is sleeping and must be awakened."

When it was Elijah's turn, he built his altar, lined up the bull, and then went full extra by soaking it all in water three times. The pit was like a mini pool, and the sacrifice was dripping more than an ice bucket challenge.

Elijah sent up a one-liner prayer, and boom, God sent down a fire that was all flex, no filter. It licked up the water, scorched the earth, and left the altar ashy. The crowd went wild, and the Baal prophets got their blue checks revoked.

Then the fire of the Lord fell and burned up the sacrifice, the wood, the stones and the soil, and also licked up the water in the trench.

After that, there was no question who was the top trending deity. The prophets of Baal were canceled, and the Israelites were hitting the follow button on God once again.

And that's the story of Elijah's Fire, where the prophet served up a divine clapback that left no room for doubt. When you bring the true God to the battle, you're always gonna come out with the win. Stay lit, fam, and remember who brings the real fire.

JONAH'S BIG FISH ENERGY

RUNNING FROM THE CALL

Jonah chapter 1

Dive into the saga of Jonah, the guy who tried to leave God on read and ended up starring in his own deep-sea adventure.

God hit up Jonah with a mission: head to Nineveh and drop a truth bomb on them. But Jonah wasn't about that life. He booked a one-way ticket to Tarshish, basically the opposite direction. Talk about ghosting divine DMs.

"Go to the great city of Nineveh and preach against it, because its wickedness has come up before me." But Jonah ran away from the Lord and headed for Tarshish.

God whipped up a storm that had the ship's crew throwing cargo overboard and praying to their follow lists. Jonah was below deck, sleeping through the chaos like someone ignoring their alarm on Monday morning.

The crew cast lots, and surprise, Jonah's the unlucky @. He fessed up and told them to throw him overboard to calm the sea. They were hesitant but eventually gave Jonah the big yeet.

Then they took Jonah and threw him overboard, and the raging sea grew calm.

God had a big fish on standby to scoop up Jonah. Inside the fish's belly, Jonah had plenty of time to reflect—three days and nights, like he was in a timeout for dodging God's call.

Now the Lord provided a huge fish to swallow Jonah, and Jonah was in the belly of the fish three days and three nights.

Jonah hit up God with a prayer that was part apology, part praise. It was the remix nobody saw coming. And God, hitting the universal unfollow button, had the fish vomit Jonah onto dry land—talk about a rough unfollow.

And the Lord commanded the fish, and it vomited Jonah onto dry land.

Post-fish, Jonah finally went to Nineveh and dropped the message. The city did a full 180, and God was like, "Mercy's the move." Jonah, though, was all pouty 'cause he wanted that fire and brimstone content.

And that's the vibe check with Jonah's Big Fish Energy. He tried to bail, but you can't outrun a God who's got the whole sea in His follow list. When the call comes in, answer it—don't wait for the fish to hit that follow back. Stay on message, peeps.

DANIEL'S LION'S DEN

TRUST LEVEL SAVAGE

Daniel chapter 6

Peep the story of Daniel, the OG believer whose trust in the Big G was so savage, not even a squad of hangry lions could shake it.

Daniel was straight vibing in Babylon, serving King Darius and slaying his government job 'cause his work ethic was next level. But the clout came with shade—other officials were jelly and cooked up a plan to cancel him 'cause of his no-cap commitment to God.

Finally these men said, "We will never find any basis for charges against this man Daniel unless it has something to do with the law of his God."

These shady officials convinced Darius to drop an executive order: pray only to the king for 30 days or get a one-way ticket to the lion's Airbnb. Daniel, though, kept his prayer routine on blast, windows open, not changing a thing.

Now when Daniel learned that the decree had been published, he went home to his upstairs room where the windows opened toward Jerusalem. Three times a day he got down on his knees and prayed, giving thanks to his God, just as he had done before.

The haters caught Daniel in 4K, praying and giving thanks to God. They snitched to Darius, who, even though he was shook, had to follow through with the law. Daniel was tossed into the lion's den, and the king was lowkey hoping for a miracle.

So the king gave the order, and they brought Daniel and threw him into the lions' den. The king said to Daniel, "May your God, whom you serve continually, rescue you!"

A stone sealed the deal, and Darius spent the night on a no-sleep grind, fasting from his usual TikToks and snacks. Come sunrise, he yeeted the stone aside and found Daniel chillin' with the lions—God had sent an angel to shut the lions' mouths. Total trust level: savage.

My God sent his angel, and he shut the mouths of the lions. They have not hurt me, because I was found innocent in his sight. Nor have I ever done any wrong before you, Your Majesty.

The king was hype and had Daniel lifted out of the den. Then, in a true plot twist, the snitches got the stitch, tossed to the lions without divine backup.

Darius went full influencer, dropping a new decree that shouted out the power of Daniel's God, turning the whole kingdom into a trending topic for the Almighty.

And that's the tea on Daniel's Lion's Den. His trust was so on point, not even a den full of apex predators could phase him. So when you're facing your own lions, remember: keep your faith on fleek, and you just might find yourself flexing in the face of adversity. Trust level: biblical.

ESTHER'S TEA

FOR SUCH A TIME AS THIS

Esther chapter 2

Listen up, 'cause we're about to spill some ancient Persian tea with the story of Esther, the queen who served looks and saved her people with some serious finesse.

Esther wasn't always royalty. She started as a regular-degular Jewish girl, Hadassah. But when King Ahasuerus was on the hunt for a new bae after yeeting Queen Vashti for the ultimate sass, Esther secured the crown with her grace and beauty—no cap.

Enter Haman, the king's right-hand man with a chip on his shoulder bigger than a TikTok influencer's ego. He hated Esther's cuz Mordecai 'cause he wouldn't bow down. So Haman plotted to swipe left on all the Jews. Major yikes.

Yet having learned who Mordecai's people were, he scorned the idea of killing only Mordecai. Instead, Haman looked for a way to destroy all Mordecai's people, the Jews, throughout the whole kingdom of Xerxes.

Mordecai caught wind of the sitch and hit up Esther with the ancient world's version of a DM, like, "Sis, you gotta use that palace clout for good." Esther was shook 'cause approaching the king uninvited was a one-way ticket to being cancelled—literally.

Esther was brave AF and invited the king and Haman to the most exclusive tea party in town. But she didn't spill the tea just yet—she was playing 4D chess, setting up for the big reveal.

At the second tea party, Esther spilled the tea for real. She exposed Haman's plot to the king, and dropped the mic with the fact that she was Jewish. King Ahasuerus was not having it with Haman and gave him the boot—or rather, the gallows.

Then Queen Esther answered, "If I have found favor with you, Your Majesty, and if it pleases you, grant me my life—this is my petition. And spare my people—this is my request."

The king was quick to flip the script. He let Mordecai and Esther write a new decree that let the Jews clap back against anyone who tried to press them. It was the ultimate Uno reverse card.

The Jews went from almost-cancelled to totally-victorious, thanks to Esther's savvy moves. Mordecai became the king's new main man, and they all lived large and in charge.

And that's the lowdown on Esther's Tea. She was the queen who came through clutch "for such a time as this," turning the tables and saving her squad. When you're feeling the pressure, remember: you might just be in the right place at the right time to serve up some piping hot justice. Stay sipping that courageous tea, fam.

#NEHEMIAH'S BUILD BACK BETTER

WALLS ON FLEEK

Nehemiah chapter 1

Grab your hard hats, 'cause we're about to witness Nehemiah, the ancient world's contractor of the year, as he gets the Jerusalem walls from busted to bougie. Nehemiah was serving Persian king realness as the cupbearer when he slid into a prayer DM with God after hearing his hometown Jerusalem was looking like a one-star review—walls down and gates burnt. His heart was on the floor, legit.

Nehemiah shot his shot and asked King Artaxerxes to let him bounce back to Jerusalem to oversee some major reno work. The king was down and even fronted the supply drop. Talk about divine favor!

When Nehemiah got to Jerusalem, not everyone was feeling the vibe. Enter Sanballat and Tobiah, the local trolls who were throwing more shade than a solar eclipse. They weren't about this wall glow-up.

Nehemiah went full stealth mode for a night mission to scope out the wall wreckage. He peeped the damage, and by dawn, he had a game plan that would make any project manager proud.

With the sun up, Nehemiah rallied the Jerusalem peeps and was like, "Let's get these walls on fleek and stop living like we lost our WiFi." The crew was hyped, and the build-back-better project kicked off.

With every brick and gate, the haters' haterade got stronger. But Nehemiah clapped back with prayer and a sword in every builder's hand, 'cause if you're gonna come for them, you best not miss.

Despite the trolls' best efforts, the wall was completed in a record 52 days. Nehemiah had those walls so on point, even the haters had to admit it was a God job.

And that's the tea on Nehemiah's Build Back Better: Walls on Fleek. He turned a rubble rumble into a fortification flex, showing us that with a squad united and a little divine backing, you can rebuild anything better than before. Stay building, fam.

TL; DR (TOO LONG; DIDN'T READ)

- **Stay Woke with Ancient Truths**: Dive into those biblical texts and you'll snag some epic life hacks. These aren't just old tales, they're the OG guides for keeping it real. Eyes open, hearts tuned in – that's how we stay woke with wisdom that's survived the ages, no cap.

- **Keeping it 100: The Takeaways:** We're all about authenticity, and these holy scripts are as authentic as it gets. They're dishing out the 411 on living life to the fullest and treating your neighbor like your squad. So here's the deal: absorb those divine deets, apply them IRL, and keep it 100. That's the path to blessings on blessings.

GLOSSARY

- **Bible**: The Good Book, God's Tweet Thread.

- **Wisdom**: The ultimate life hacks.

- **Prayer**: Sliding into God's DMs.

- **Miracle**: Epic win by the Big G.

- **Faith**: Trusting the process, no WiFi needed.

- **Sin**: Epic fail, needs divine ghosting.

- **Repentance**: Saying "my bad" to the heavens, hitting the reset button.

- **Salvation**: Get that eternal VIP pass.

- **Commandments**: The OG 'terms and conditions' for living right.

- **Prophets**: The legit inside scoopers from way back.

- **Psalms**: Holy Spotify for the soul.

- **Testament**: The two-part epic series of divine deets.

- **Old Testament (OT)**: The classic throwbacks, full of origin stories and major plot twists.

- **New Testament (NT)**: The sequel with all the Jesus content and how-to-live-right guides.

- **Creation**: The Almighty's glow-up for the universe. Day 1 to Day 6, He was on a roll, no cap.

- **Eden**: First-ever crib, where humans ghosted God's 'no apple' rule.

- **Noah's Ark:** The OG survival kit – big boat, big flood, big save.

- **Moses**: Dude who left Pharaoh on read and dipped with the Israelites.

- **David and Goliath**: Underdog story where small squad beats big mood.

- **Prophecy**: Spoilers for humanity, but make it holy.

Printed in Great Britain
by Amazon